i do

Designed by NVU Productions. Distributed by NVU Editions. Printed and bound in the
United States of America.

ISBN 0-9724575-3-4

JESSICA SIMPSON *i do* ACHIEVING YOUR DREAM WEDDING

Concept by Tina Simpson. Written with Katina Z. Jones. Designed and edited by NVU Productions.

PHOTOGRAPHY BY JOE BUISSINK, ASHLEY GARMON, AND CRISTIANA CEPPAS.

to Nick, my love. —JS

foreword

JESSICA SIMPSON

When I was a little girl, I often dreamed about my wedding day. The bedtime story of my childhood was Cinderella. Although it was a fairy tale, I knew that one day I would have my own story of love to share.

As you turn through the pages of my experiences, I hope that you are enchanted, but more importantly inspired by true love. Loving my husband was never meant to be a private emotion. I believe that when you are truly in love, you want to climb to the top of a mountain to shout out your emotions so the entire world can smile upon your blessing.

Planning your wedding can be both exhilarating and exasperating. It is an experience you hold next to your heart for the rest of your life. As a bride-to-be, I was extremely calm because I wanted to take in every moment to cherish. It is so easy to get caught up in the stress of it, because there will be things that don't happen according to plan. Trust me, I know.

But when those double doors open to everyone you love standing up in awe, and your eyes are fixed upon your "Prince Charming," there is no greater feeling possible. You find your peace.

My wedding wish for each of you as you embark upon this journey is to simply enjoy every moment.

It is absolutely the most amazing day of your life.

My Love
Jessica Simpson, Trina Harmon

The deepest of your love is my love
The promise of your life is my life
Wherever you go, I will follow
Where your head lays, I will stay
Until my dying day

Always you and I, my love
Always your tears I'll cry, my love
If ever one soul was meant for mine
I have been blessed by the kiss of a lifetime
Always I'll praise the skies, my love
For my love

Everything I am is your love
And every day I live is for your love
Wherever I go, you follow
Where my head lays, you stay
Until my dying day

Always you and I
Always I'll praise the skies, for you
For my love

Jessica Simpson
BRIDE

Nick Lachey
GROOM

the dream makers

Achieving a dream wedding doesn't happen by itself. It takes calculated planning, inspired creativity, and a clear vision of the final goal. These are the in-demand professionals who helped Jessica bring her ideal wedding to life. Draw from their rich experience, and use their practical advice to create an event that people will remember even as you toast your golden anniversary.

Bride Jessica Simpson is a pop music recording artist with a five-octave range. Her albums (*Sweet Kisses, Irresistible,* and the brand new *In This Skin*) showcase not only her talent but also her uniquely charming and very romantic personality.

Look for Jessica's personal reflections throughout the book.

Groom Nick Lachey is a successful recording artist who made his mark on the pop music scene with the group 98° before releasing his new solo album. He called his October 2002 wedding "the most incredible day of my life."

Tina Simpson
MOTHER OF THE BRIDE

Joe Simpson
FATHER OF THE BRIDE

Ashlee Simpson
SISTER OF THE BRIDE

Jessica's mother, Tina Simpson, provided immeasurable support throughout the wedding planning process, often meeting with vendors to personally oversee arrangements.

Look for Tina's personal reflections throughout the book.

Joe Simpson, Jessica's father and manager, has always had a special bond with his oldest daughter and is a strong shoulder to lean on.

Ashlee Simpson, Jessica's sister and maid of honor, plays Cecilia on the WB's *Seventh Heaven*.

Mindy Weiss
WEDDING COORDINATOR

Mindy Weiss is one of the most sought-after party planners in Southern California. She and her memorable events have been featured in *InStyle, Martha Stewart Weddings, Modern Bride, People*, and *Town & Country*.

Joe Buissink
PHOTOGRAPHER

Joe Buissink is an award-winning photographer based in Los Angeles. He has photographed weddings all over the world. His work has been featured in *Gourmet, InStyle, People*, and in the book, *The Wedding Box* (Rizzoli, 2000).

Vera Wang
FASHION DESIGNER

Celebrated New York fashion designer Vera Wang created Jessica's customized traditional strapless dress, and the gowns of dozens of celebrity brides, including Toni Braxton, Kate Hudson, Debra Messing, Melissa Rivers, and Uma Thurman.

Sam Godfrey
PASTRY CHEF

Sam Godfrey is well known for his unique and delectable special occasion cakes. Based in San Francisco, Sam has created cakes for Oprah Winfrey and has been featured in *Brides, InStyle*, and *Town & Country*.

Mark Held
FLORIST

Mark Held is owner of Mark's Garden in Los Angeles. Among his star-studded list of clients are Gwen Stefani, Charlie Sheen, Tom Arnold, and Kimberly Williams.

Ken Pavés
HAIRSTYLIST

Los Angeles-based hairstylist Ken Pavés is the genius behind Jessica Simpson's simple yet luxurious wedding hairstyle. Other clients include Jennifer Lopez, Celine Dion and Cameron Diaz.

Rita Hazan
HAIR COLORIST

New Yorker Rita Hazan is the colorist responsible for Jessica's natural-looking baby blonde hair. Like her colleague Mr. Pavés, Rita has worked with such personalities as Jennifer Lopez and Celine Dion as well as Kim Cattrall and Carmen Electra.

Karan Mitchell *left*
Ulli Schober *right*
MAKEUP ARTISTS

Makeup artist Karan Mitchell, of the Los Angeles-based Luxe Agency, has worked with stellar beauties such as Naomi Campbell, Catherine Deneuve, and Rebecca Romijn-Stamos.

Makeup artist Ulli Schober at Celestine in Los Angeles created the radiant look of Jessica's skin on her wedding day.

Jessica Paster
PERSONAL STYLIST

Jessica Paster is the personal stylist to several celebrities, including Jessica Simpson, Cate Blanchett, Naomi Watts and Minnie Driver.

Melissa Bozant Washington
MANICURIST

Melissa Bozant Washington owns Epicureus Petite Spa in Beverly Hills and offers brides a Seche™ Kit for healthy, natural-looking nails.

first things first

first things first

For recording artist Jessica Simpson, it all began with a romantic dream. As a little girl in Texas, she had written dozens of letters in her diaries to the "dream man" she knew she would one day meet and marry. Her mother kept all of these letters; from those etched with crayons to those carefully crafted in teenage prose.

Who knew that one day Jessica would be presenting her "prince" with a framed version of one of these heartfelt entries—a letter entitled, "To My Future Husband"?

On October 26, 2002, at the Smith Family Chapel of the Riverbend Church in Austin, Texas, Jessica married her true love, recording star Nick Lachey of 98°, in a flower-filled candlelit ceremony attended by more than 250 guests. They had met four years prior, and Jessica quickly discovered that Nick was the man for her. "My knees got weak, and he totally took my breath away. I was totally, completely in love from the start." For Nick, it was also love at first sight, and after a few years of dating, the two finally united in marriage.

There was romance in the air on that October wedding day, down to the last detail. A heartfelt song, "My Love," written by the bride for her groom set the mood. A candlelit hallway with photographs chronicled the bride and groom's best times together. A perfectly sculpted five-tiered wedding cake provided a stunning focal point. Elegant white candles, fragrant gardenias, and countless pink blush rose petals made the breathtaking picture complete.

But, like all weddings, this one had its challenging moments, such as an unexpected Texas rain. In the eleventh hour, tents and fabrics had to be rented to convert the ballroom into the idyllic setting wherein Nick and Jessica would celebrate their first moments together as husband and wife.

Weather aside, it was a day that Jessica still refers to as "magical." In the photographs capturing the magic, you'll see her calm, ecstatic glow in every moment—and the creativity and care that went into every detail.

TO MY FUTURE HUSBAND In the nervous excitement before the ceremony, Nick opened a present from his soon-to-be bride. Written before they met, the letter was taken from seventeen-year-old Jessica's diary, affirming their love and commitment.

starting from scratch

HOW TO BEGIN
PLANNING THE WEDDING YOU'VE ALWAYS WANTED

FEEL LIKE A PRINCESS With the help of Carol Brodie at Harry Winston, Jessica was fortunate enough to have more than one majestic option for her wedding headpiece. Pictured above is a 34-carat diamond tiara. Her final choice was an 11-carat pavé diamond headband that was specially attached to her custom-made veil.

FALLING INTO PLACE Flowers. Venues. Rings. There are countless details involved in wedding planning, and seemingly endless decisions to be made. When it's done right, everything falls into place to create an experience that truly reflects the couple's personalities.

Setting the date

Setting the date for your wedding can seem, at first, to be the simplest thing in the world. After all, you've waited your whole life for the right person to come along, everything after that should fall into place. But the truth is, setting the date can be as complex as an algebraic equation. You'll need to be sure your date of choice doesn't coincide with holidays, family occasions, church or synagogue events, or even your work schedules.

Choose the day of the week carefully. Most guests cannot attend weddings in the middle of the week. Faith comes into play as well; Christians tend to shy away from Sunday weddings, while people of the Jewish faith typically don't choose Saturday nuptials.

Since many traditional wedding and reception sites tend to be booked at least a year in advance, you would do well to look for sites that are off the beaten path. Get creative: how about a riverboat, the beach, or a snow-covered mountain range? Think about places you both enjoy, and then set your date based on location.

Nick and I are very busy people, but we were lucky that our schedules allowed for a fall wedding. That's what I wanted from the very beginning— it's my favorite time of year in Texas.— JS

We had a lot of family and friends we wanted to invite, and we needed time to help plan their travel arrangements. Also, our first choice for the reception didn't work out because the University of Texas was having its homecoming that weekend. Timing is crucial when you're planning a wedding.—TS

NO JOB TOO SMALL Care goes into every detail, even triple-checking the spelling of each individual guest's name.

CONSTANT CONTACT Jessica's wedding planner, Mindy Weiss, kept a watchful eye over the proceedings throughout the entire day, and kept in touch with key players via walkie-talkies.

calling in the experts

With so much emotion and so much to do, it's hard to keep from feeling overwhelmed. That's why many brides-to-be hire professional consultants to help them create the wedding of their dreams. A good wedding planner can help you coordinate everything from where to have your engagement party to thank-you letters after the event—all within your predetermined budget.

A good wedding planner can help you coordinate everything from where to have your engagement party to thank-you letters after the event—all within your predetermined budget.

As with any professional, good communication is essential, and it all starts from the initial interview. Beverly Hills-based wedding and party planner extraordinaire Mindy Weiss was the mastermind behind Jessica's wedding. She says there are five questions you should ask your party planner:

1 | How many weddings do you work on per year?
A party planner that does mostly proms or bar mitzvahs may not be right for you.

2 | Will you be at my event or will you send an associate?
You may become attached to your planner, only to be shocked to see her assistant on your wedding day.

3 | Are you willing to use the caterer or photographer that I've chosen?
You want a planner who will give you what you want, even if it's not her first choice.

4 | How available will you be?
Some planners are more accessible than others. If you want to reach them at a moment's notice, say so early on.

5 | Can you meet with me outside of business hours?
Many brides and grooms work, so evenings and weekends need to be part of the deal.

Finally, ask yourself, "Do I like this person?" You are going to be spending a lot of time with your wedding planner. Personality is important.

INTERVIEW WITH WEDDING COORDINATOR *Mindy Weiss*

Taking the legwork—and the worry—out of the entire wedding planning process is Mindy's unique talent. "I handle all the details," says Weiss, "so the bride and groom can concentrate all their love and attention on each other. They trust me to know all the options, to have excellent resources totally at my fingertips, and to step in where they need negotiating power."

Weiss coached, advised, and represented Jessica and Nick on everything from site selections to menu planning and showers. "We looked at six locations before we decided on a golf resort in Austin. There were other sites that were appealing, but they couldn't provide the service and security necessary for a wedding of this caliber."

Upon meeting Mindy, I immediately connected with her. She understood exactly where I was coming from. — JS

Weiss alone was responsible for many of the finer details of the Simpson-Lachey nuptials: a palatial fabric-draped ballroom; rose petals down the aisle; a dresser featuring candles and framed photos of Jessica and Nick in various moments throughout their relationship; elegant place settings with menus tucked neatly into napkins. These are the kinds of finishing touches that Weiss is known for. They create an even more memorable celebration for family and friends.

How can you achieve this kind of ambiance at your wedding, without breaking the bank? "Make wise choices," advises a savvy Weiss. For starters, buy flowers that are seasonal and readily available—then use more greens as filler. "Jessica's dream was to have hundreds of pale pink roses, which were not seasonal, so it cost a significant amount more to ship them in for the wedding," says Weiss. "As an alternative, achieve a soft, romantic look by using lots of candles instead of more flowers. If you want fullness on the bottom of a table arrangement, you can use more candles there, too."

I tagged along with Jessica and Nick while choosing the wedding planner. It was ultimately their decision, but I knew I would be communicating often with whomever they chose—and I loved their choice! — TS

Weiss is a fan of eclectic vases of differing sizes, shapes and colors. She and her assistants collect vases especially for use in sophisticated weddings, then place the unusual finds on the wedding party and guest tables. On a shoestring? Check out thrift shops, estate and even yard sales. You never know what treasures can be found where you least expect them.

The best part of being a wedding coordinator is that I am fortunate enough to create lifetime memories.—MW

"Stay away from the cookie-cutter look as much as possible," offers Weiss. "People like to be able to move around and look at different items on tables and unusual points of interest." For Jessica and Nick's reception, one of the more unusual points of interest Weiss created was a low wrought iron fence covered in flowers to surround guests on the dance floor. Another warm touch was the Chiavari bamboo chairs with gardenias, custom-designed for the wedding party.

EACH SETTING UNIQUE Symmetry is nice in some cases, but don't get mired in making sure each table is exactly the same. Weiss used eclectic, mismatched candleholders to give the reception hall a soft, romantic look.

PERSONAL MENUS To add an unexpected but very personal touch, use a good laser printer to create personalized menus for each guest.

A WARM GLOW Fire's natural light softens any mood. Jessica's wedding had hundreds of candles scattered throughout the reception room.

SIGNATURE ACCENT Due to unexpected rain, this impromptu guestbook table was set up on a dresser, featuring photos of the couple throughout their relationship.

KEEPSAKES Jessica and Nick gave each guest a CD of the two songs they had written for each other.

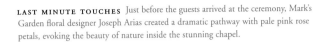

To replicate looks like the dance floor fence, Weiss suggests you go to Home Depot, purchase some affordable picket fencing and paint and create the look you want. "Be sure to check with the reception site first to be certain it's okay to bring a fence into the facility prior to the wedding—and be sure you have some folks on hand to set it up for you. Don't be afraid to be creative, to ask for what you want. Since you're the one paying for the event, it really should be everything you dreamed of."

Make wise choices such as buying flowers that are seasonal and readily available. Jessica's dream was to have hundreds of pale pink roses, which were not seasonal, so it cost a significant amount more to ship them in for the wedding.—MW

Of course, not every budget allows for a wedding planner, but you can still take some great advice from the experts. Weiss offers brides these tips on how to "be your own wedding planner":

Set a realistic budget so you know how and where to distribute your money.

Create a "Wedding Planner Notebook" to stay organized. Keep notes and pricing from every vendor here.

Delegate specific tasks to trustworthy friends and family, such as setting up seating cards, contacting all the hired vendors to give them your expectations the day of event, and calling them again the day before to confirm arrival.

On the day of the wedding, appoint a person to be by your side to handle any last-minute needs and to manage the schedule. This person should be familiar with all of your family's and friends' assignments.

A Wedding Planner's Survival Secrets

Don't expect perfection—if you do, you will undoubtedly be disappointed. "There is no possible way to be perfect, so let go of that and just have fun," advises Weiss.

That said, do go into the whole process with confidence that everything will be beautiful and memorable.

Include both sides of the family in the entire process. "With the Internet, you can now scan and e-mail dress and floral designs, site photos and even cake plans," says Weiss. "It's a good tension-reliever, and it adds so much warmth and unity when the whole family feels involved."

Stay calm. "When you're calm, you can allow everyone around you to do a better job," says Weiss. "Let go, let it happen—and keep your sense of humor."

Remember the groom. "Most grooms tend to be relaxed," says Weiss, "but they may still need help getting ready. Every once in a while, I get one with the jitters, and the best way to calm them down is to keep them informed about how everyone else is doing."

Take an emergency kit with you. Weiss' emergency kit for brides includes aspirin, lotion, breath mints, fabric tape, Band-Aids™ and scissors.

Beware of hidden costs. Says Mindy, "If you're not having your wedding at a hotel that supplies the tables, chairs, and dishes and you're trying to find a unique location, the rentals can blow you right out of the water. Understand that you have to bring in everything from salt and pepper shakers to bathrooms. So keep that in mind when balancing your budget against a location.

SPECIAL DELIVERY 30,000 pale pink roses were shipped to the wedding from California, because they were out of season in Texas. It was no small task for florist Mark Held and his designer Nancy Kaye to coordinate the shipment and set them all up in a matter of hours.

photography

When you think about the countless moments that create a spectacular wedding, it's easy to want every single one to be captured on film. The truth is, with so much going on, it's not humanly possible for your photographer to frame every second of the day's events. You'll definitely need a photographer who understands how to choose the images that will best bring the memories to life.

Your first step in choosing a photographer is to talk to other recent brides within your circle of family and friends. Who did they most enjoy working with, and why? Look through their photo albums and try to find a style that's compatible with your personality. Do you want to have elegant, stylized black-and-white photos, or would you prefer to remember your day in living color? As you can see throughout these pages, Jessica and Nick decided they wanted both black-and-white and color photographs to commemorate their big day. If you, too, decide you want both, you should make sure to see the photographer's entire portfolio. Interview many photographers with as many different styles as possible—don't just look at standard portrait photographers.

RADIANCE One of Jessica's favorite photographs was this portrait, taken with an infrared lens. Joe also captured a tender moment between the groom and his mother.

CONTEMPLATION Through all the hectic excitement, neither Jessica nor Nick lost track of what's really important. During the rehearsal dinner, in the brief "calm before the storm," the couple shares a moment of quiet prayer.

Another thing to consider is the type of photography you want. Keep in mind that the half hour or so of posed pictures following the ceremony is not necessarily the most important aspect of the photographer's job. Candid shots of the bride, groom and their close family and friends interacting when they're not posing for the camera can make for keepsakes that really tell the story of your wedding. Think about what you want before you meet your photographer, so you can be as specific as possible with your instructions.

TASTE TEST The newlywed couple were the first to sample Godfrey's creation. They confirmed that the cake truly did taste as good as it looked.

"Ultimately, I was so honored to be able to do this cake for Jessica and Nick. They had heard about Perfect Endings through a mutual friend in the recording industry, Walter Afanasieff. I had created his groom's cake in the shape of a piano and included edible sheet music. His bride, Cristina, recommended me to Jessica for her wedding."

For Jessica and Nick, Godfrey created an outstanding five-tiered cake with buttercream icing and an elegant flowered topping, perfectly complementing all of the other design elements of the wedding. "The cake needs to look like it belongs in its environment. It was traditional, yet sophisticated, polished yet romantic."

For those on a budget, Godfrey has several key recommendations:

Consult with cake makers early in the planning process so that you have a realistic idea of how much cakes cost before finalizing your overall budget.

The wedding cake should be the sole dessert, and you should choose a cake maker who is as renowned for the taste of their cakes as they are for the design. You get more for your money when the cake is worth eating. You'll want to avoid at all costs having a wasteland of uneaten cake slices scattered around the reception site.

Choose buttercream instead of fondant. Not only does it taste superior but it should be at least several dollars less per serving. In warm weather have the cake delivered, completely decorated and assembled, later in the day to prevent melting. A grand entrance by an exquisite cake adds a wonderful touch of drama to your special day.

Choose a rich cake with intense flavors such as chocolate, coffee or hazelnut. People will be satisfied with a smaller piece, and it will not appear as if you are skimping.

Most of all, Godfrey advises, don't be afraid to try something new. For example, one recent innovation in wedding cakes is Perfect Endings' signature cupcake tower, a trend that has become popular as a modern-day wedding tradition. "Be creative," says Godfrey. "It's your day, so don't be afraid to express yourself."

Showers and Gifts

MARK THE OCCASION WITH MEMORABLE CELEBRATIONS
PRIOR TO THE BIG DAY

Celebrating with Showers

Showers have come a long way from their traditional pasts. Today's showers are often planned around themes or focus on a specific element. However much they've changed, though, showers always were and still are parties with a specific purpose: to help the happy couple fill their nest with all of the items that they'll need in their new life together.

There are as many types of showers as there are couples, but some of the more popular ones include: Recipe/kitchen, Bath, Lingerie, Bedroom, Linen, Garden, Entertainment, Personal (e.g., massages, spa treatments, etc.).

Showers always were and still are parties with a specific purpose: to help the happy couple fill their nest with all of the items that they'll need in their new life together.

Your bridal party—and often your maid or matron of honor—will often make the appropriate choice for your shower. If you have any specific requests in the way of a theme (such as a theatrical New York-style shower or an outdoor Southern-style picnic), tell your maid or matron of honor as soon as possible to allow enough time for proper planning.

Most showers include a simple menu of lunch or dinner and dessert, party favors, a door prize and perhaps an interesting game or two to break the ice between people from both sides of the family who are meeting for the first time.

Of course, you can choose a simpler, more casual event such as a barbecue—or something more formal, like a tea party—to help guests get to know each other before the big day.

Whatever theme or type of shower you choose, the most important thing you can do is relax and have fun. Ask one of your bridesmaids to take photos or videotape the event, and have yet another help you with thank-you notes as soon as the event is over. That way, you'll have less on your mind as the big day draws near.

BRIDAL LUNCHEON Jessica's bridal luncheon was hosted by three aunts and allowed her a special opportunity to thank each of her attendants personally. A unique element was that each guest brought a charm that represented their relationship or memory of Jessica, then presented them individually.

LINGERIE SHOWER Since Jessica's absolute favorite food is Tex-Mex, she chose Rosie's Tamale House for her lingerie shower. After great food and margaritas, Jessica opened her intimate—and sometimes hilarious gifts.

Jessica and Nick's Garden Party

Several weeks before the wedding, Jessica's close friends got together and threw her and Nick a lovely shower at a beautiful home outside of Dallas, Texas. The casual garden party was held in a backyard, complete with a tent setup for guests to dine under. The evening presented Nick with a unique opportunity to meet some of Jessica's friends for the first time.

Gifts were bestowed on both the bride and groom-to-be: Jessica received many of the kitchen and china pieces she had registered for, while Nick (who had registered at Sears and Home Depot) was gifted with all kinds of great tools, and workout and gardening equipment. It was a great opportunity for family and friends to gather and give Jessica and Nick gifts that they knew they would appreciate both individually and together as a couple.

> It was so nice to spend time with our friends from Texas, who we don't get to see very often. They went all out on this event for Jessica and Nick and made it very special to them.—TS

> The lingerie shower was so much fun because it was all of my best girlfriends together—some of whom were meeting for the first time. It was a good way to relax and spend time with my girlfriends for the last time as a single woman.—JS

Girls' [Last] Night Out

Another memorable shower Jessica had was a lingerie shower held at a Mexican restaurant just outside of Austin. It was given by a group of six of Jessica's friends, but her sister Ashlee, with the help of Los Angeles party planner Pamela Yeager, coordinated everything from the bus ride to the restaurant to the racy bachelorette party afterwards.

The sixty or so guests arrived in Austin and were taken by chartered bus to Rosie's Tamale House, a colorful and vivacious Mexican restaurant, for dinner, dessert, and the ceremonial opening of the gifts. The centerpiece of the shower was a voluptuous pink-icing bustier cake from family friend Carol Reid of Dallas.

> A family friend made the cake for Jessica's lingerie shower. I thought the pink bustier was just so Jessica, and just perfect for the day. It matched her invitation, down to the lace.—TS

Gifts included soft, silky negligees and satin undergarments, but several were hilariously funny. Although he wasn't there for the lingerie shower, Nick wasn't completely forgotten—some of the gifts were actually for him! The evening culminated in a girls-only bachelorette party at a club in downtown Austin, with cocktails, revelry, and entertainment, the details of which have yet to be revealed by Jessica or any of her guests.

GENEROSITY Some people prefer to ship gifts to your home before the wedding, but more often guests bring their gifts to the reception. Appoint a trusted friend or family member to arrange for their safe transportation at the end of the night.

the gift-giving tradition

It's okay to admit it: one of the more enjoyable decisions you get to make as a couple is choosing the items you'd like on your wedding gift registry. Picking out the things that will make your house more of a home can actually be a wonderful way to blend your styles and solidify the bond between the two of you. From rugs to toasters to the "good" china, piece by piece you will build more tangible evidence of a strong foundation for your newlywed home.

When you read about the elaborate (and often unusual) wedding gifts bestowed upon celebrity couples, you might wonder how you can provide eclectic choices for your wedding guests without seeming ostentatious. But just because you might want some unusual gifts doesn't mean they have to be expensive.

Here are some tips to help you make gift giving easier for your guests:

Show some personality. Your choices should reflect who you are as a couple. If you are both creative types, opt for funky flatware and colorful stemware. Subtle colors are classic choices for the more traditional couple. Some people choose not to register for formal china or silverware at all. Don't be afraid to show who you are by the choices and gift suggestions you make.

It was fun to have Nick there to open our first wedding gifts together, seeing all of the wonderful things we had registered for, and knowing they came from special people in our lives.—JS

Register for a variety of items. This allows guests to choose gifts of different price ranges, and shows courtesy on your part by not limiting guests to high-ticket items that might be out of their budget range.

Let people pitch in. Some larger stores offer a service where several guests contribute a small portion toward a large-ticket item such a coffee table or a couch. Similarly, some travel agencies allow guests to contribute a portion of the couple's honeymoon expenses. This way, several guests can "pitch in"—without much planning on their part.

Leave the gift certificate option open. Let guests who are either too busy to shop or overwhelmed by selection have the option of purchasing a gift certificate for you. These especially come in handy after the wedding, when you've opened all your gifts and discovered that some necessary items are missing.

The Internet has made it easier than ever for couples to register their wish lists online—and retail websites have made it even easier for guests to shop for and purchase gifts online as well.

You can also register the old-fashioned way—in person at your favorite department store. This is a good option when you are unsure of what you might want, and need some personal assistance from an experienced clerk. Typically, the department store uses a computerized system to enter all of your gift choices, making it easy for guests to enter your name or date of wedding and immediately access a list of items still needed. In some cases, the in-person registry will also show up on the store's website.

the pleasure of y...

at the marriage of thei...

Jessica Ann S...

to

Mr. Nicholas Scott...

son of Mr. John Scott...

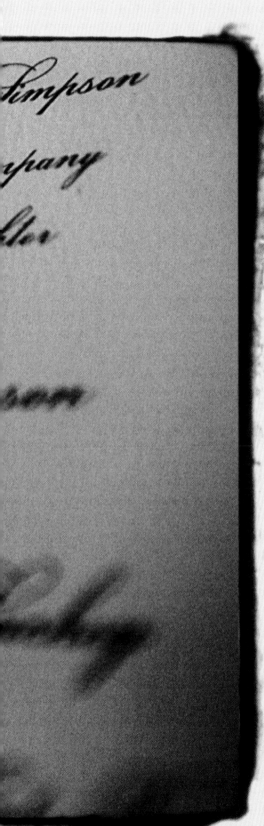

the Written Word COMMUNICATE WEDDING DETAILS
TO YOUR GUESTS WITH A PERSONAL FLAIR

FIRST IMPRESSION The invitation is the first chance for your guests to experience the tone of your wedding, so make sure it is in keeping with your theme.

LESS IS MORE With all of the options of paper styles, weights, fonts, and textures, it's easy to be overwhelmed. Remember that simplicity can often make a classic, elegant statement.

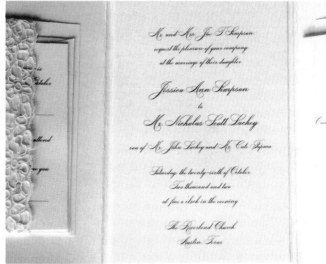

Choosing the right invitations can seem at first glance to be one of the more mundane tasks in the grand scheme of wedding planning. Just a few years ago, most brides had to visit printers' offices to begin the highly uncreative task of choosing from a small selection of preprinted samples and templates, without any possibility of adding their own personal style.

Spreading the News

With hundreds of invitation styles, sophisticated papers and computerized templates now readily available, your wedding invitations can truly convey the essence of your personalities. They can be signature pieces that set the tone for the entire event and its festivities.

Mindy Weiss helped us with our invitations, and they looked so elegant with a sheer satin bow around each one. They really set the tone for a sophisticated wedding, and played out the wedding's theme of lace and romance.—JS

There are countless techniques for creating invitations. Some of the most common are: fabric (embroidered silk with coordinating ribbon), photographic design, sheer overlay (translucent vellum paper over the printed invitation), formal engraved, botanical (with pressed flowers), letter-pressed, monogrammed, layered, vintage, and laser cut (with intricate, even lace-like designs).

For an even more personalized approach, consider working with a stationery or graphic designer to create an invitation that's uniquely yours. But remember that some specialty papers are much more expensive than others, so set a budget early in the process to keep costs in check.

We got so many wonderful comments about the invitations from our guests. They especially liked the personal touch of including a quilt square—on each, they were to write their best wishes for Jessica and Nick. They sent these in with their RSVPs. A quilt was made and was displayed at the reception.—TS

Avoid ordering too many or not enough invitations, and be sure to proofread invitations carefully. Consider the etiquette of naming everyone correctly, especially when parents of the bride or groom are divorced.

One final note: Contrary to what you might hear, remember that you don't have to follow the rules if you don't want to. Ultimately, the invitation sets the tone for your wedding, and it should be an expression of you as a couple, so try to create a theme that you both are happy with.

One of the nicest new wedding trends is the addition of a printed program to guide the guests through the ceremony. These lovely printed pieces introduce guests to all of the wedding's participants, from the bride and groom to the bridal party, minister or officiant, and vocalist or musicians.

Capturing the moments of your special day has been made easier than ever with computerized templates—many of which are available for free download off the Internet. Using a predetermined format, you can easily input your personal wedding details into the document, then print it on nice parchment paper, roll it into a scroll and tie it with a ribbon that matches the colors you've chosen for your wedding. Or find a nice cover stock, have a calligrapher create a monogram, and bind it to your wedding program with ribbon or zigzag stitch from a sewing machine.

Creating a Program

Wedding programs are especially helpful to out-of-town guests who may not know everyone from both sides of the family.

Wedding programs are especially helpful to out-of-town guests who may not know everyone from both sides of the family. They also offer a terrific opportunity to publicly thank your parents or family for all their hard work in bringing you to this moment.

Keepsakes and Well-Wishes

Months or even years after your wedding, you'll want to remember who was in attendance—and what better way than to create your own customized guest book? It can be as simple as purchasing a blank Guest Book and having guests sign it, but it's also nice to include places in the book to add photos taken from cameras left on each table. You can also leave a blank journal on every table so that each guest can jot well wishes in his or her own personal style. Another creative option is to provide a Polaroid™ camera by the guestbook, and ask guests to leave a picture of themselves along with their names and wishes.

Encourage your guests to write a wish, piece of marital advice, or a favorite anecdote about the two of you as a couple. You may choose to do this in the guestbook or separately, on pieces of paper or a large piece of cloth hanging on a wall. Special thoughts like these will help you enjoy your happy memories, and may also help you realize strength in the challenging days ahead. Later on, you'll be happy for this special source of inspiration and support.

Whatever you decide, leave lots of room for your guests to do more than just write their names. This keepsake will become one of your most cherished possessions as a couple, so you'll want it to be as complete as possible.

QUICK THINKING Wedding planner Mindy Weiss did such an amazing job setting up the impromptu (due to rain) guestbook area, that even the bride herself couldn't believe it was planned at the last minute.

PERSONAL MENUS Mindy Weiss created these personal menus by running cream colored paper through a laser printer to create a simple but elegant detail for each guest.

SEATING ASSIGNMENTS Organizing the seating for a 300-guest wedding is no small feat, especially when the reception is moved indoors at the last minute. Make sure whoever is in charge of seating has the organizational skills and attention to detail to make it work.

Seating arrangements

Planning a peaceful, intimate wedding reception can often depend on how well you plan seating arrangements. Seating Aunt Mabel next to Uncle Paul, her eternal nemesis, might cause your blissful evening to erupt into World War III.

Ask your wedding planner to help you organize the seating charts. If you are doing the planning on your own, enlist the help of friends and relatives. The easiest way to plan seating is to obtain a blank seating chart from the reception site, enlarge it using a photocopier, and fill it in using a pencil to allow for plenty of erasing. Find out from your parents or other relatives where they would like to sit and with whom, then plan close friends' seating arrangements, and finally plan where everyone else is to be seated.

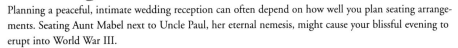

You can't please everyone, but you can create an air of class and consideration by arranging seating in ways that best position your guests for a happy and relaxing celebration.

Allow for a few extra seats, or perhaps an open seating area toward the back of the reception site. You can't please everyone, but you can create an air of class and consideration by arranging seating in ways that best position your guests for a happy and relaxing celebration.

For Jessica's wedding, Mindy Weiss made mini menus instead of place holders—and tucked them neatly into napkins on plates. This was a nice, delicate touch. It looked great, but was really inexpensive.—TS

Once your guests are assigned to tables, you may choose fun, personalized ways to help them find their seats. For instance, you can place small potted plants near each plate, with place cards on Popsicle sticks. Or, make place cards using labels from your computer, stick them onto colored pieces of cardstock, punch a hole in the card and tie the place card around the stemware at each place setting. The possibilities for place cards are limitless, so be creative, and have fun with it.

the night before

PREPARING WITH YOUR FAMILY AND FRIENDS
TO MAKE THE MOMENT PERFECT

REHEARSAL Regardless of where you have your actual wedding ceremony, there will most likely be a rehearsal the night before. This gives everyone involved in the wedding a chance to walk through the sequence of events to practice their roles for the next day.

Rehearsal dinners

Your rehearsal dinner is a great time for everyone in the family and wedding party to meet each other, and is also the official kickoff to the wedding festivities. The groom's parents often host the dinner, but you and your fiancé may choose to host the dinner instead.

Your rehearsal dinner should have a decidedly different mood, style and menu than your wedding. If your wedding is a formal sit-down dinner, then a casual, relaxing rehearsal dinner would be the perfect complement. Opt for foods that are different from the wedding menu—you don't want to serve the same dish two nights in a row.

Jessica and Nick chose a nautical theme and chartered a boat complete with a Texas-style barbecue buffet and line dancing—all reflecting Jessica's Texas background. The guests enjoyed the casual atmosphere, fantastic food and down-home style of the festivities.

Lots of brides and grooms are getting creative with themed rehearsal dinners such as a Mexican fiesta, a Hawaiian luau, a New England-style clambake or a Western barbecue. For their rehearsal dinner, Jessica and Nick chose a nautical theme and chartered a boat complete with a Texas-style barbecue buffet and line dancing—all reflecting Jessica's Texas background. The guests enjoyed the casual atmosphere, fantastic food and down-home style of the festivities.

Of course, if you'd prefer to stay traditional, there's always the formal sit-down dinner at a nice local restaurant. Often, restaurants have rooms that work well for private parties. Call ahead to ask the restaurant to feature hors d'oeuvres; ask that the first hour of the rehearsal dinner be a casual "happy hour" where your guests can walk around and mingle before dinner.

Formal invitations for the rehearsal dinner are not necessary, but you might send a note with directions to the restaurant, especially if some members of your wedding party are from out of town.

Invite all those who will take part in the wedding ceremony to the rehearsal dinner, including spouses or dates of all adult attendants, in addition to your parents and grandparents. You can also invite other family members who are not part of the ceremony and out-of-town guests to join your rehearsal dinner as special guests. It's great to spend more time with your family and out-of-town guests, especially since you may not see them very often.

I wanted it to be a big "hoedown," so that everyone could get a feel for some down-home Texas-style hospitality. I chose a pink Prada dress and pink boots, but the most fun thing was seeing Nick in his first pair of cowboy boots. It was so cute how he kept stepping on my feet when we were dancing.—JS

Add a personal touch to the evening by including several photos of yourselves through the years; it's fun for your bridal party and relatives to see how you evolved from children to the adults who you are today. For dessert, many couples choose to serve the groom's cake at the rehearsal dinner. If you have time, you can also make or buy small favors to place in a basket at each table.

The rehearsal dinner is a good time to review any last-minute details with your family and wedding party—not everyone knows where and when they are supposed to meet the next morning, and this is a good time for them to have any questions answered.

This rehearsal dinner was such a hoot—from the campy bandanna-inspired invitations to the line dancing, it was a blast from beginning to end.—TS

Have a great time, but don't forget to go easy on the alcohol and get a good night's sleep—tomorrow is the beginning of your new life together!

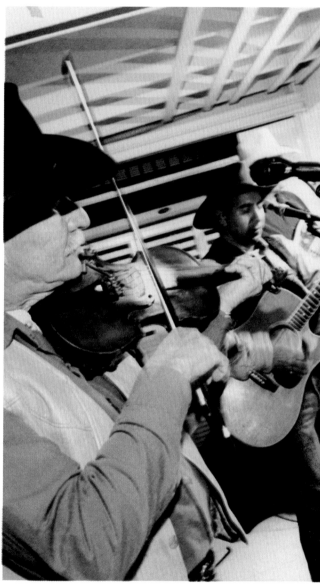

SUNFLOWERS EVERYWHERE For Jessica and Nick's rehearsal dinner, Mark's Garden went with a more informal and fun theme, using bright colored hydrangeas and vibrant sunflowers arranged in galvanized metal pails. These set the perfect mood for guests to relax and enjoy each other, while keeping the atmosphere bright and playful.

THE BAND A local Austin bluegrass band kept revelers on their feet throughout the cruise.

WARM GLOW Yellow and red candles added a warm glow to the interior of the boat, matching the lively, colorful theme.

BOOT SCOOTIN' Since the invitation called for "country chic," the groom wore his first-ever pair of cowboy boots. His bride forgave him when he stepped on her feet!

MOONLIT NIGHT Jessica and Nick agreed—the cruise was a stunning, and yet relaxing evening; the perfect preface to their wedding day.

THE REACTION Although many brides present their gifts at the rehearsal dinner, Jessica chose to give each of her bridesmaids a personalized gift at the bridal luncheon, on the day before the ceremony.

Showing appreciation

The best way to say "thank you" to your wedding party for all their love, help, and support is to give them a small token of your appreciation in the form of a personalized gift.

Some unique gift ideas include gourmet cooking classes; monogrammed accessories (necklaces, purses, and wallets); necklaces you've made by hand; gift baskets, including spa treatments, journals, or stationery. For the guys, try monogrammed belts, tool kits, key chains, or handkerchiefs.

No time for personalized gifts? Try a gift certificate—it allows your wedding party to choose the gift that is right for them. One idea for an off-the-beaten-path gift is the "dinner-and-a-movie" gift certificate— which you can pull together quickly using gift certificates from a local restaurant and movie theater.

I gave each of my bridesmaids a belt, bracelet, and T-shirt with each one's first initial on it, and included drawer sachets too.—JS

The best way to say "thank you" to your wedding party for all their love, help, and support is to give them a small token of your appreciation in the form of a personalized gift.

Most often, the wedding couple bestows thank-you gifts upon their attendants at the rehearsal dinner, but you can choose a bridesmaids' brunch or bachelorette and bachelor parties as the right time to give bridesmaids and groomsmen their gifts.

As a final, personal touch, consider saying a few words about each attendant as you offer their gift. Anecdotes or funny stories about your times together would also be appropriate in moments like this, so have some fun with your mini-speeches!

Jessica wanted this time to be special for each girl who was involved in her wedding. She wrote precious letters to each one expressing how much they meant to her. It was very sweet, and very Jessica.—TS

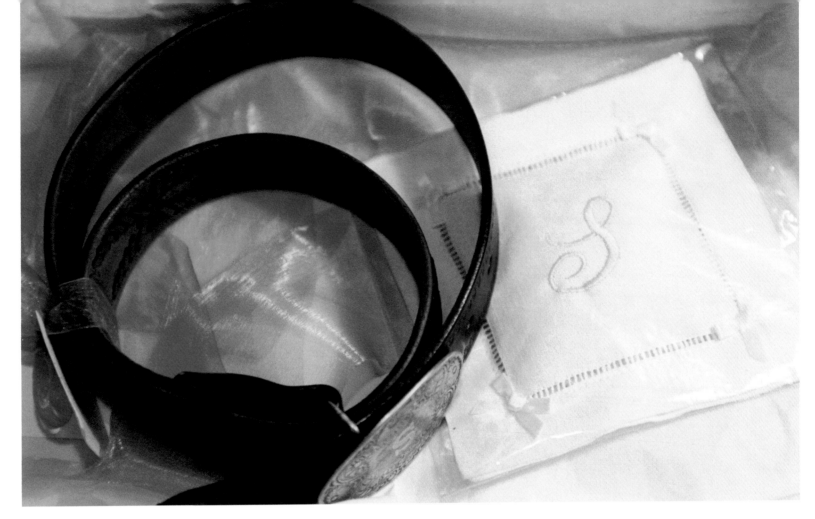

TEXAS HOSPITALITY The unique belt, sachet, and T-shirt given by Jessica to her bridal party were the result of another great tip from wedding planner Mindy Weiss. It was a personal gift that reflected Jessica's background while expressing her creativity and care.

O happy day

O happy day

October 26, 2002, was a special day for Jessica and Nick, not simply because it was the day of their wedding. It was also a day that seemed like forever in coming. From a little girl's love letters to her one-day "prince," to years of dating and discovery, to months of intricate, well-choreographed planning, this event was the most highly anticipated day of the couple's lives.

How does an event like this really come together? Mostly under the direction of the wedding planner. "Mindy Weiss really pulled all the details together," says Tina Simpson. "Whenever something went wrong, or wasn't what we had hoped for, Mindy saw to it that there was an immediate resolution. Throughout the day, she made everything just right for Jessica and Nick."

With meticulous attention to detail in everything from décor, cake, and flowers to vows, music, and a rousing reception, it's no wonder that Jessica was relaxed and glowing on her wedding day. "I had complete confidence in Mindy and what we had planned," says Jessica. "She knew what we wanted and was able to make it all come together beautifully. We had the most romantic wedding I've ever seen."

STEALING A KISS Between the wedding and the reception, Jessica and her new husband shared a kiss together. "Overwhelmed with happiness" is how Jessica described her feeling at that moment.

getting involved HAVE THE PEOPLE WHO MEAN THE MOST
PLAY A ROLE IN YOUR WEDDING DAY

BONDS OF FRIENDSHIP Jessica's childhood friend Brian Buchek, now an ordained minister, performed the wedding ceremony, despite the fact that Jessica's dad, Joe, is also a minister. She wanted her dad to just relax and be part of the wedding, and since Brian was there from the beginning of Jessica and Nick's relationship, he was a natural choice.

Performing the Ceremony

The wedding ceremony is the most important moment of the entire day, so use care in choosing who will officiate or perform the ceremony.

A special ceremony conducted by someone who you know and trust can really set the tone for a more meaningful day. So often, this choice is put off until too late in the planning stages. Many brides are told that the minister from their church is the only person who can marry them, so they aren't aware that they have a choice in the matter.

Here are some things to think about when choosing the person who will marry the two of you:

Is this the kind of person you're looking for? You may want an officiant who is a traditional priest or rabbi, or maybe a judge or mayor, or a nondenominational minister. Whichever you choose, be sure that the celebrant is legally authorized to consecrate a marriage.

Do you trust this person? If not, you may be more nervous on your wedding day than you need to be. Good chemistry between the three of you makes the ceremony run smoother.

Brian Buchek is one of my best guy friends. We used to have late-night talks about everything, and there wasn't a doubt in my mind that he'd be perfect as our minister. He's so articulate and incredible with his words. He really made people understand the love that Nick and I share.—JS

Will the officiant allow you to write your own vows? If this is important to you, make sure you secure this agreement well ahead of the ceremony.

Can the officiant marry you in the location of your choice? If you want a backyard wedding and your minister or rabbi is unwilling to officiate such a wedding, you'll need to consider another person (or location).

Finally, you should attend at least one other wedding at which the officiant presides. You'll want to get a good sense of what this person looks and sounds like to others, and how you feel when you're a guest. A strong, capable officiant will make guests feel welcome, and put the entire wedding party at ease.

SISTERLY LOVE Jessica's younger sister Ashlee was a natural selection for maid of honor. The two have always been close and share a special sisterly bond.

family matters

Having a large bridal party on a small budget isn't usually an option. So what can you do if you have several close friends and large families on both sides?

To make sure no one in your family gets left out, there are several creative options for having family members participate besides being in the actual bridal party:

Ask the male members of your family to be ushers instead of having the groomsmen do it. Most weddings have at least one usher for every 25 guests.

There are many traditional roles for family and friends who aren't in the main wedding party. For them, inclusion in your special day may be as simple as reading scripture passages during the ceremony or toasting the bride and groom at the reception.

Ask younger family members to stand outside the church to welcome guests. They can hand out programs, and even flowers for the female guests.

I wanted my sister to be standing close to me as I was up there making my vows, since she's the one who's been closest to me all of my life.—JS

Have a designated guest book attendant. Choose someone outgoing and creative, so they might offer helpful suggestions to get guests started writing anecdotes or advice.

Ask older friends and relatives to help with baking or as personal assistants to your wedding party. If you can't afford a professional wedding planner to manage your event, designate one or a few people to serve as assistants, complete with checklists and emergency kits (for sewing, makeup, hair and more).

Keep the memories alive. Bridesmaid Lea Lachey, co-owner of party planning company Signature Soirees, suggests wearing a ring that belonged to a departed loved one, or sewing it into the inside of your dress. Jessica wore her grandmother's ring on her right hand as a way of keeping her close to her heart on her wedding day, and the Bible used in the ceremony belonged to Nick's recently departed grandfather, Robert.

Ask one or two people in your close circle to find a creative way to include any missing family or friends. Perhaps they can do a small table of photos with a small flower arrangement, or read their letters of congratulations at the reception.

There are many more traditional roles for family and friends who aren't in the main wedding party. For them, inclusion in your special day may be as simple as reading scripture passages during the ceremony or toasting the bride and groom at the reception.

A final option might be to present a brief slide show or video depicting the bride and groom throughout the years. This can be a touching, even hilarious, tribute to the bride, groom, and their families.

BRIDESMAIDS From left to right, Jessica's bridal party was Lea Lachey, Jessie Rice Holliday, Andrea Lee, Lesa Neff, Jessica Cooper Melker, Ashlee Simpson, Robin Johnson Webb, Stephanie McGuire, and Lisa Christensen.

FLOWER GIRLS The two flower girls are Kia Henson (4 years old) and Meghan Goodlett (3 years). Their fathers, Andre Henson and Jay Goodlett, are both groomsmen.

GROOMSMEN From left to right, Nick's groomsmen were Justin Jeffre, Devon Biere, John Lachey, Tony Christensen, Gavin Gleason, Andre Henson, Jay Goodlett, Brian Bonecutter, Drew Lachey, and Isaac Lachey (front row).

RING BEARER Devon Biere's 4-year-old son Nick was the ring bearer (far left, front row).

SHARING JOY Formerly bridesmaids in each other's weddings, Tina and her sisters Debbie Hering and Connie Smith share a memory and a laugh after the ceremony.

GRANDPARENTS OF THE BRIDE A.E. and Dorothy Drew danced the night away at the reception. Jessica's grandparents had wise words of advice on how to make a marriage last.

GRANDMOTHERS OF THE GROOM Leigh Fopma and Ruth Lachey smile on their grandson's new happiness.

PROUD PARENTS Nick's father and stepmother, Nick and Iris Lachey, welcomed Jessica warmly into their family.

MOTHER OF THE GROOM Kate Fopma, Nick's mom, shared her son's feeling of joy at the reception.

Making the most of it

BEING PREPARED SO THAT YOUR DAY
IS EVERYTHING IT'S MEANT TO BE

QUIET EXCITEMENT Jessica was extremely calm, but she was also quite excited by the thought of seeing Nick, and of having Nick see her in her wedding gown. She says it seemed like forever between the night before and the actual wedding ceremony.

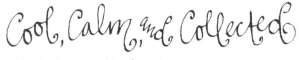

Cool, Calm, and Collected

Your wedding day is finally here, and it's the happiest day of your life. There's just one thing distracting you: your frazzled nerves. There are many things you can do to reduce your stress level and calm your nerves well in advance of the Big Day:

Get lots of rest. Most brides-to-be have so much on their minds working out final details of the wedding that they find it difficult to sleep. Make sure you get enough.

Get some exercise. Keep your heart pumping steadily in anticipation of the big event. Even going for short walks can help you burn off some excess nervous energy, not to mention keep you looking great in your dress!

Eat breakfast. Many brides are too nervous to eat on the day of their weddings, but it's important to eat small amounts of healthy food throughout the day to stay energized.

I wanted everyone to be very relaxed on my wedding day, so we all went for a spa treatment the day before the wedding while the guys played golf. It helped us feel so fresh and relaxed.—JS

Drink lots of water. Nothing is better for your body than eight 8-oz. glasses of water per day. It's great for your skin as well.

Try aromatherapy. Calming scents such as peppermint, chamomile and jasmine can help relax you when you're feeling tense or anxious.

Take a bath. If your energy's feeling spent from the night before, the best way to reclaim it is with a warm, mineral sea salt bath. It's invigorating and energizing, yet helps you to remain calm and relaxed.

Jessica was so unbelievably calm on her wedding day. She even had the presence of mind to be able to write a special letter to Nick. Everyone commented on how happy and relaxed she seemed all day long.—TS

Talk it out. If you are feeling like you might lose your composure, find one of your attendants and have a good, long talk. This is the reason you chose your bridesmaids in the first place: to have trusted helpers and confidantes to support you through one of the most emotionally intense days of your life.

Finally, remember to breathe. Deeply and frequently throughout the entire day. It's easier said than done, but in truth, there's no better relaxant than some good deep breathing. Make sure to remind yourself as often as possible to relax, take a deep breath, and let yourself enjoy this wondrous day.

HEARTFELT WORDS In the last moments before the ceremony, Jessica wrote a tender letter to Nick, then sealed it with a kiss. He received it just before the ceremony began.

romantic details

For romance to be "in the air" on your wedding day, you can fill your church and reception site with all the flowers and candles money can buy. But ultimately, true romance is in finer details such as personal notes, happy smiles, and small gifts that share your love with your guests. Here are Jessica's tips for making the most of your wedding day:

Sometime in the weeks prior to the wedding, write a letter to your new mate, dated for your wedding day. This will become a treasured keepsake, and will remind you both of all the reasons why you are tying the knot. In your letter, you can thank your new husband for all the wonderful things he is to you: lover, friend, protector, and inspiration. Make it from the heart.

Nick and I had promised each other that we wouldn't spend much on wedding gifts to each other, since we were already spending our money on our wedding. When he received the framed letter I had written to my "Prince," he was really excited and emotional.—JS

Collect a few dozen of your favorite quotes, stories, or poems about love. Print them neatly on pretty parchment paper, with your names and wedding date on the back. Punch a hole in them and tie them to each guest's wine or champagne glass with a soft silk ribbon. This will go a long way toward making your guests feel the spirit of your love, and it will make for a lovely favor and keepsake.

Sometime in the weeks prior to the wedding, write a letter to your new mate, dated for your wedding day. This will become a treasured keepsake, and will remind you both of all the reasons why you are tying the knot.

Make or purchase hand-painted dishes or wine glasses with your wedding date on them, and leave them at each table as a special memento for each guest. Every time they use this item in the future, they will think of you and your happy day.

Create a simple gazebo for your wedding reception out of materials from a local fabric or craft store. Place it in the middle of the dance floor for a more intimate first dance. Just make sure there's still enough good lighting all around for your photographer to be able to effectively capture these moments.

Spend less on other aspects of your wedding in order to splurge for a romantic carriage ride. You might also opt for a strolling violinist, a quartet or a jazz guitarist at your reception as opposed to a band or a DJ. This, too, would make for a cozy, intimate and very romantic wedding celebration.

Whatever you decide to do to create romance, be careful not to overdo things. Less is always more when it comes to romantic extras on your wedding day.

the look of love

HOW TO BE BREATHTAKING
AS YOU WALK DOWN THE AISLE

SOMETHING OLD Ken jokes that stylist Jessica Paster, who was lucky enough to secure some vintage Van Cleef hair clips worth thousands of dollars, would hold him personally responsible for the entire cost if anything happened to them.

Crowning Glory

Great hair doesn't happen on its own. But if you spend a bit of time in advance coming up with the perfect look, you needn't spend a lot of money on your hair the day of the wedding.

HAIR PERFECTION Celebrity hair wizard Ken Pavés knew exactly what to do with Jessica's hair for the wedding, and was especially mindful of the fact that Nick likes Jessica's hair down in full romantic style.

You can start your search for your "perfect look" by combing through the pages of hair and bridal style magazines. Pay attention to length and color. What stands out to you as being beautiful? Keep a journal or wish list with hairstyle photos and detailed notes about what you like and don't like, then share it with your stylist to provide the most accurate picture of the style you're after.

Most professionals recommend coming in months ahead of time for a few trial runs on haircuts and color. Try out anywhere from two to six 'dos before you say "I do" to one.

Here's more advice from the pros on hair styling:

Plan well ahead of the big day. Don't wait until the last minute to try a radically new look. It could be too hard to recover from, and you might wind up feeling very "un"-you.

Spend as much time as you can working with your stylist to come up with a few different options. We tried several looks before determining our direction, but I ultimately trusted Ken and Rita to make it look fantastic. You need to have that level of trust with anyone who works on your hair, even if it's a friend.—JS

Talk to your regular stylist, or find a new one. If you wouldn't trust your tresses to anyone but your regular stylist, stick with the tried-and-true, but if you've heard of a good stylist who specializes in bridal hair, it might be worth a visit to his or her salon. Also, ask if the stylist would be willing to come to your home on the day of the wedding to perform any last-minute miracles, if needed.

Work within a hair-care regimen. Don't just shampoo and condition your hair in the weeks before the wedding; get your hair in its best-ever shape. Try some hair-revitalizing vitamin supplements from a health food store or hot oil treatments, especially if your hair is dry and brittle from coloring and perming over the years. Don't forget to drink lots of water. This helps you grow healthy, new hair by removing toxins.

Don't overdo it. Using too much product (perms, color, sprays and even shampoo) can damage your hair, making it difficult to style.

Jessica's hair looked so amazing throughout the entire day. I never had any doubts about Ken and Rita taking care of her. They've both worked with Jessica for years, and always make her look so beautiful.—TS

Between one and two weeks before the wedding, **spring for a deep conditioning treatment to rev up your hair and pump up its volume.** Deep conditioning also leaves hair feeling remarkably soft. If you're on a budget, home kits are available where you simply need to massage the conditioner into your hair and cover it in plastic for a few hours.

If you do your own hair color, do it well ahead of the wedding. Even if it's only a retouch job, give yourself a couple weeks for the color to blend in and for natural moisture to return to your hair and scalp.

The main goal of your pre-wedding hair-care regimen is to accomplish everything but final styling in the days prior to the event, so that your hair stands the best chance of holding its style through what promises to be a long, happy, and incredible day.

INTERVIEW WITH HAIR STYLIST *Ken Pavés*

AND COLORIST *Rita Hazan*

One of the most critical members of a celebrity's team is a good stylist, and Jessica's is on the A-list for many of Hollywood's elite. Celebrity hairstylist Ken Pavés of Pavés Salon & Spa (with salons in Los Angeles, Chicago, and the Detroit area) says working on Jessica's hair was a breeze because she has such an easygoing attitude. "We kept Jessica very much herself in terms of hairstyle," says Pavés, "and she was very confident in her own look."

Pavés says that since Jessica was a young bride, he styled her hair so that it wasn't "too serious or too done. Wedding hair should be confident and comfortable, and we styled Jessica's the way Nick likes it best: long and pretty."

In keeping with the wedding's romantic theme, Pavés gave Jessica's hair the look of spun silk, with a natural wave pattern and expensive jewels sewn into her hair. "She had two flame-shaped brooches on the side and one in the back," says Pavés. "Everything about her hair was magical."

Pavés used a curling iron and a volumizing aid to create spiral curls that he later loosened into finger curls. He finger-combed the curls out with a laminate gloss and then sewed the jewels in to complete the wavy, romantic look. "To create the same look for less," offers Pavés, "you can sew in rhinestones. These add an instant element of glamour to your hair."

To keep the finished look in place, Pavés suggests using a quick-dry spray versus a very wet hair spray. For naturally curly hair, you should polish the curls so they don't look too frizzy.

Ken is one of my best friends in this industry. He's incredibly sought after, and yet always makes time for me. He's one of the funniest guys I've ever known, and I couldn't have had this day without him.—JS

"Jessica is one of my favorite celebrities to work with because she is so positive and upbeat. I helped her with my own conditioners and styling ability, but in the end it was the bright light within her that made for a perfect style. I took a lot of photos of different styles, and left them with her to decide which one looked best."

COLOR MATCH Rita Hazan did Jessica's hair color the day before the wedding, and she also did coloring for Ashlee, Jessica's grandmother, aunts and three bridesmaids the day of the wedding.

Even the best haircut and style needs to be highlighted. That's where Jessica had some extra help from seasoned New York hair colorist Rita Hazan, who has provided a stunning glow in the hair of high-profile celebrities like Jennifer Lopez.

"Jessica's a natural blonde, so we just put in pale blonde highlights to give her more of a 'baby blonde' look," says Hazan. "This lightens up her color and makes it more golden. This was a really natural look for her wedding day."

From the moment we first met, Rita and I immediately clicked. Nobody can do color the way she does. A lot of colorists can really damage your hair, but Rita brings out the most naturally beautiful golden colors in my hair. I love her work.—JS

Some of the bridesmaids had hair color that needed a boost, and Hazan was there to care for them as well. "You really need everyone looking their best, but most of all they need to look natural and blend in with the group."

The more natural, the better. You want to look back at the pictures years later and think that everyone still looks naturally beautiful. Pictures are forever, and every bride should look beautiful, not funky or trendy, on her wedding day.—RH

Hazan suggests that the bridal party first concentrate on keeping hair healthy in the weeks before the wedding, then try to match hair color to their skin tone, versus experimenting with exotic shades. "The more natural, the better. You want to look back at the pictures years later and think that everyone still looks naturally beautiful. Pictures are forever, and every bride should look beautiful, not funky or trendy, on her wedding day."

Hair color should also accentuate dresses. "Jessica's hair was remarkable because it complemented her dress, and the dress complemented her," says Hazan. "Everyone in the wedding party showed me photos of themselves in their dresses, and then had a color consultation prior to the week of the wedding."

Hazan suggests finding a good professional to help you with hair color ideas at least two months before the big day. "This way, you have time to make changes if they are needed. You may need a touch-up right before the wedding, but once you've got the look down, last-minute maintenance becomes so much easier."

CANVAS Ken always keeps Jessica laughing with his great sense of humor. He even has a name for his wig model, which has a different face drawn on each side of her head. "Watch what you say around Canvas," he jokes. "She's two-faced."

JUICY DETAILS Juicy Couture, one of Jessica's favorite clothing lines, sent her this fun outfit as a surprise. Jessica had a nightmare just before the wedding that her dress didn't show up, so she was forced to walk down the aisle in the hoodie and sweatpants. Luckily, this dream didn't come true!

AN ARTIST'S TOUCH Ulli knew exactly what to do for Jessica in terms of her wedding makeup. All Jessica really wanted was a dewy, shimmery glow—a look that was easy for Ulli to accomplish.

the face of beauty

You'll never want your look to be more perfect than on your wedding day. This is your chance to shine— but don't let your makeup outshine the natural beauty of your skin. This isn't the time for high drama in the form of heavy mascara, bright glossy lipstick, and super rosy cheeks. Rather, it's a time for subtle, accentuating cosmetics that enhance and support your natural beauty.

Remember that your "look" should reflect your personality. You shouldn't stray too far from your natural appearance—after all, your spouse-to-be is marrying you for the person you already are.

Hiring a makeup artist can be a fun and helpful way to discover your natural glow, and it needn't be too expensive. There are several ways to find an artist who can help you better show off your inner beauty on your wedding day:

Visit a cosmetics counter or day spa to book an appointment with a makeup artist or consultant. These professionals are trained in the art of subtlety, and can help you discover new ways to wear your makeup. A good makeup artist is skilled in minimizing problem areas while maximizing your more positive features. This professional should also be very experienced in lighting and photography, in order to best prepare your face for the hundreds of photos that will be taken throughout the day.

If you feel you can do it yourself, go on a makeup-buying expedition and try new shades or hues on different days to see which ones look better on you. Don't be afraid to ask for samples. They're a great way to test out new products.

Contact a local Avon or Mary Kay® representative. Often, these independent reps are more than willing to help with bridal party makeovers, as long as you purchase some products from them.

Ask a friend who always seems to have perfect makeup to be your honorary makeup artist. Go out to lunch and make a girls' day of it!

Remember that your "look" should reflect your personality. You shouldn't stray too far from your natural appearance. After all, your spouse-to-be is marrying you for the person you already are. Think of your bridal makeup as merely an enhancement.

ULLI AND KARAN Jessica's wedding makeup was the handiwork of two of Los Angeles' top makeup artists, Ulli Schober (right) and Karan Mitchell.

INTERVIEW WITH MAKEUP ARTISTS *Ulli Schober* AND *Karan Mitchell*

Perfecting Jessica's harmonious glow on her wedding day was easy for makeup artist Ulli Schober of the Los Angeles-based Celestine Agency. "Jessica is such a natural beauty, so I stayed away from anything too heavy and focused on accentuating with very soft sorbet colors that enhanced her natural glow," says Schober, who primarily used NARS™ brand cosmetics for the entire Simpson bridal party. "I began with a foundation that included moisturizers, then mixed in a soft glow, and used minimal powder. On her eyes, I used shell pink and a soft apricot with gold mixed in, accentuated with a smudged sable brown eye pencil to soften the finished look."

Schober recommends starting with the eyes and working your way down to cheek and lip applications. "This way, you won't smudge your eye makeup, and your cheek and lip colors won't get smudged as you're dressing. Also, you should definitely groom your eyebrows days before the wedding to avoid puffiness or redness, avoid strong colors in eye shadow, and use a waterproof mascara to avoid smearing when the tears begin to flow later in the day." Schober believes strongly that well-groomed eyebrows are the key to well-accentuated eyes.

Both Ulli and Karan are amazing with color and technique. They make you look beautiful naturally. Having them there made everything complete.—TS

Creams, beiges, and pinks are universal shades, so Schober highly recommends sticking with classic color choices such as these for eye shadow versus blues and purples, which she says tend to photograph poorly. Your color choices should also reflect your skin tone and not your hair color. For instance, African-Americans might choose more berries and deeper apricots, while Asian brides might opt for apricots over pinks. All should stay away from reds, blues, and purples, which are too dramatic for such a romantic day.

Mascara can be black for all in the wedding party except those with blonde hair and blue eyes. Those types are better off with a warm brown mascara that isn't as dramatic as black.

For Jessica's cheeks, Schober used a very soft blush powder mixed with warm apricot and a peachy pink undertone. She applied the apricot first, and then added the peach and pink to the apples of Jessica's cheeks for a fresh, glowing finish.

I love to have them around me, because they make my whole day better.—JS

Jessica's lips were given a dreamy look that nicely complemented the wedding's theme of elegant romance. "I started with a light beige touch-up stick to line the outside edge of the lips, which opens them up, making them appear bigger and softer. You can use a touch of foundation with a brush to achieve the same illuminating effect." Schober did not use a lip liner on Jessica's lips, but rather let them stand out with great color choices such as washed-out berry and soft pink. She discourages the use of gloss: "It's off in a second, and it can be distracting," she says. "You can use it for photo shoots, but not for the actual wedding ceremony. If you are going to use gloss, choose transparent or pearl over intense colors." To keep lip color in place, Schober advises that you blot with tissue paper and use loose powder in between layers of lipstick.

ASSEMBLY LINE While Ulli did Jessica, Tina and two bridesmaids' makeup, Karan worked on six other members of the bridal party. Everyone's makeup was picture perfect in just under three hours.

Bridesmaids can customize their eye shadow according to their dress colors, skin tones and eye colors, more so than is appropriate for the bride. But Schober recommends that they stay within the same color family for a more finished, consistent look. "No one should overpower the bride," she says. For all brides and bridesmaids, Schober suggests a good facial with lots of moisturizing "at least a week before the wedding. Very clean, moisturized skin is the best starting point for a fresh, wonderful look. The more you prepare your skin, the better it will look. Less cosmetics and more healthy skin is ideal for any wedding party."

Schober advises makeup moderation as a good rule of thumb. "For instance, when I created Jessica's foundation, I mixed in a very small dab of pearl color to give a soft, dreamy shine to her face," says Schober. "If you mix in too much, you can wind up looking too oily. Too much powder can make your face look too dry. Use glow judiciously. Put some on the outer side of your cheekbone to create a soft, fresh look."

As a final tip, Schober suggests brides designate one bridesmaid to carry the all-important makeup purse, and perhaps an additional friend to be the official "makeup artist."

For the cost-conscious who might not be able to afford a trip to the day spa before the wedding, Schober offers the following skin-care tips to whip your skin into great shape:

Shred up a cucumber and use it as a moisturizing treatment.

Steam your face over a bowl of hot water.

Purchase makeup based on color choices, not expense (she recommends the "inexpensive yet lovely" Sonia Kashuk™ cosmetics available at Target stores nationwide).

Mix a small amount of body glow into body lotion before application to create a subtle, all-over glow.

Use a plate for mixing colors or glow so that you can see how much you're using, then apply with fingers or a small cosmetics spatula.

Karan did me the biggest favor—she made my bridesmaids feel and look like Hollywood glamour stars.—JS

As a final tip, Schober suggests brides designate one bridesmaid to carry the all-important makeup purse, and perhaps an additional friend or family member to be the official "makeup artist." This way, you won't need to worry about where your makeup is, and what condition it's in by the end of the night, since this makeup artist will be keeping tabs on your look from start to finish. "Weddings are long events," says Schober, "and you'll want someone to touch up your look throughout the day."

Karan Mitchell, the makeup artist from L.A.'s Luxe Agency who worked with the bridesmaids and Nick's mother, agrees with Schober's natural beauty tips. "We wanted a soft, bronzy glow with minky taupe eyes and soft lips to complement the champagne-colored dresses," she says. "But even though it looked unified, it wasn't cookie-cutter. It was a harmonious look with a definite theme of romance and subtlety."

Mitchell softened the lips of each member of the bridal party by using lipstick first, followed by lipliner and a coat of gloss. "It was a stylized look where less was definitely more," she says. "The biggest challenge was getting it all done in three hours!"

Mitchell's best advice for the bridal party is to tack on an extra hour ("everything takes longer than you think on the wedding day"), have a good game plan for getting everything done, and purchase decent-quality makeup. "You're going to have the wedding pictures for a long time, and you want to look timelessly beautiful."

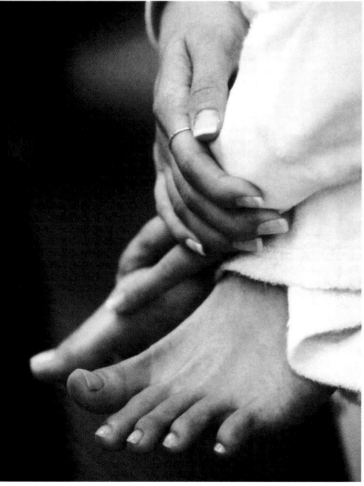

SIMPLE ELEGANCE Ms. Washington lends a hand to the bridal party, making their nails beautiful. Clockwise from left: Ashlee, Tina, and Jessica.

nailing it down

In all the excitement that surrounds your wedding day, it's possible that you might have forgotten an important detail: your nails. Planning ahead can help you achieve a clean, well-manicured look.

Don't think no one will notice if your nails don't make the cut. Remember that one of the star attractions at your wedding (besides you, of course) is your wedding ring, so many people are going to ask to see your hand on your wedding day.

Here are some tips for you and your attendants to have healthy, beautiful-looking nails for this special occasion:

If you are going to opt for acrylic nails, get them done at least a week prior to the wedding. Keep them at a fairly conservative length. Long, decorated nails are not appropriate for weddings.

Ask your bridesmaids to keep their nails in classic style (not too long or too short) with a soft shade that is not overpowering or distracting.

Suggest that your groom get a manicure as well. Some men may shy away from this, but ask him to consider that his hands will be featured in many of your wedding photos. They shouldn't look too rough.

If you're planning to go with your natural nails, start working on getting your nails in shape at least four to six weeks before the big day. This should give your nails a chance to be healthy and strong.

Don't forget hands, arms and feet. They need the spa treatment every bit as much as your nails. Your nails won't be as pretty if the skin around them is dry or scaly.

Opt for a pedicure if you are having a summer wedding, or if you are planning to honeymoon on the beach. You'll want your toenails to be as lovely as your fingernails. They should also be either the same shade, or one that's just a shade or two darker than your fingernails to be in keeping with your soft, romantic look.

From exchanging rings to cutting the cake and waving goodbye, your hands and nails are going to be in the spotlight from start to soft finish. Since manicures can be inexpensive, it would be well worth it for you to invest in having your nails professionally done for your wedding. Think of how lovely your hands will look in your photographs!

INTERVIEW WITH MANICURIST *Melissa Bozant Washington*

Beverly Hills-based celebrity manicurist Melissa Bozant Washington, who owns and operates Epicureus Petite Spa in Los Angeles, has perfected the nails of Jennifer Lopez, Reese Witherspoon, and Meg Ryan. Washington is known for offering her clients indulgent, artistic experiences in therapeutic hand and foot care. For Jessica, she provided her full six-week Seche™ regimen, beginning with a microdermabrasion hand and foot bath to smooth skin on Jessica's hands, arms, and feet.

Jessica's lovely, natural nails were first given a base coat of Seche™ pearl, then painted in a Seche rose nail lacquer. "Her nails looked very natural, but they had just the right amount of shine for the photographs," says Washington.

Melissa was so great to work with, because she really takes her time. She knows exactly how to make nails look perfectly natural and beautiful. I think having gorgeous hands and nails can give brides a real boost on their wedding day.—JS

Washington suggests that brides do their nails in a natural pink, and then coat them in a complementary soft, baby pink. "It blends right in when you polish them," says Washington.

If you can't afford the star treatment for your nails, you can replicate Jessica's look by following Washington's simple tips:

Buy a basic exfoliator (usually about $5). Use it to soften elbows, hands and feet in the weeks before the wedding.

Do mini-manicures several times in the final few weeks. Push back cuticles, then use oil and nail strengthener to ensure that your nails will be in the best possible shape. Follow up with a daily hand cream.

Jessica's nails were perfect. Melissa really made her hands glow every bit as much as her skin.—TS

Purchase a nail-care kit from a professional manicurist to be sure you have all the right products to help you keep your nails in shape. Washington's Epicureus Petite Spa sells its Seche Kit for $25 (see Resources for contact information).

the Magic Moment THE ANTICIPATION OF A LIFETIME
LEADS TO TODAY

MAGICAL RAIN Although most brides stress out at the mere thought of rain on their wedding day, Jessica took it all in stride. Her attitude reflects the wise words of her wedding planner, Mindy Weiss: "Don't think of rain as a disaster. Think of it as an unexpected surprise. Rain is magical."

MOMENT OF PEACE Jessica shares a quiet moment of prayer with family and bridesmaids before her journey down the aisle.

from dream to reality

It's finally here. Your wedding day has moved from dream to beautiful reality. You're flooded with emotion, and can't help but have a few doubts. Will everything go exactly as planned? Is there anything you've forgotten? Will your guests actually show up?

It's easy to get wrapped up in worries on your wedding day, but take comfort in the fact that it's perfectly normal for a bride to be nervous. It would be out of the ordinary if you weren't. The best thing you can do is remind yourself that everything has been taken care of, and that some things that you didn't plan are going to happen anyway.

I was not nervous, I was just anxious. This was the moment when Nick was finally going to see me in my dress, and it was something I had dreamed about for a long, long time.—JS

So, get focused. Stay calm. Take a deep breath, and get ready for the most memorable day of your life.

At 5 p.m. on October 26, 2002, Jessica Simpson and Nick Lachey were married in an intimate candlelit ceremony attended by 300 of their family and friends. The ceremony was held in the smaller Smith Chapel of Riverbend Church in southwest Austin, Texas, tucked neatly into the hills near the Colorado River. The scenery was outstanding. However, the weather left a little bit to be desired. It was overcast and misty, a bit more suitable for umbrellas and raincoats rather than sunglasses and cameras. Still, this wedding was one to behold: romantic, intimate and very personal. It was everything Jessica had dreamed of since she was a child, and that made her new husband Nick especially happy.

The couple exchanged vows, lit their Unity Candle, and then, in a euphoric state, strolled back through the crowd of well-wishers while a 25-voice gospel choir sang, "O Happy Day."

At the lavish reception at Austin's Barton Creek Resort, guests dined on Maine lobster bisque, spinach salad with candied pecans, and lemon-thyme chicken breast with wild mushroom polenta.

Guests hit the dance floor to the energetic music of Austin band Big Time, which played all of Jessica and Nick's favorites, along with some unexpected surprises. A DJ also supplied music, keeping the guests partying long into the night as the newlywed Jessica and Nick disappeared off to their honeymoon.

All told, it was a magical evening—a fairy-tale ending to a pop princess' lifelong wish for the prince she always knew would come.

Ceremonial tradition

Jessica and Nick's wedding ceremony was very traditional in that it followed the sequence of events and schedule typically seen in Christian weddings:

3:15 p.m. Wedding party dressed and ready for pre-wedding pictures.

4:30 p.m. Wedding party ready to begin ceremony.

4:40 p.m. Soloists/musicians begin selections.

The ceremony itself can vary, of course, depending on the couple's religious affiliation. Most commonly, there are initial remarks by the celebrant, followed by readings and hymns and then the wedding vows. Many religious ceremonies include a blessing of the rings and end with a public pronouncement of the couple as husband and wife. At Jessica and Nick's wedding, the officiant asked for God's blessing on the newly married couple as they began their new life together.

Of course, you can deviate from the more traditional ceremonial events. Just be sure to get approval from the church or officiant well in advance of the wedding.

4:45 p.m. Guests are seated by the ushers, groomsmen, additional family members or friends. (Note: Seating typically begins with the bride and groom's grandparents and parents.)

5:00 p.m. Processional begins. The officiant and the groom typically enter from the side of the church. Bridesmaids are escorted down the aisle by groomsmen, followed by the maid/matron of honor and best man. The ring bearer and flower girl come down the aisle just before the bride and her father (or other specially designated person).

5:10 p.m. Wedding March begins, and the bride is given away to her new husband at the front of the church.

saying "i do"

Many traditional churches have their own wedding ceremonies that are commonly performed, but with good planning and communication up front, you can almost always add your own personal touch to the ceremony with vows you've created together.

You can create vows from using your favorite lines of love poetry, or simply sit together and pour your thoughts about your commitment onto paper. What do you ultimately wish to give to each other, spiritually and emotionally, for the rest of your lives? What does marriage really mean to you? Anything that speaks positively and eloquently to your intentions would make an appropriate and lovely addition to your personalized wedding ceremony.

If you want to share your vows with your guests, you might consider printing them on the back of your wedding program. This leaves your family and friends with a lasting souvenir of your wedding, and will be a meaningful addition to your wedding album.

If you want to share your vows with your guests, you might consider printing them on the back of your wedding program. This leaves your family and friends with a lasting souvenir of your wedding, and will be a meaningful addition to your wedding album.

One word of caution: if you want to be married using your own vows, be sure to consult with the officiant well in advance of the wedding ceremony. Some churches prefer particular vows in their ceremonies and may be hesitant to do anything other than the tried-and-true.

OLD FASHIONED LOVE Jessica and Nick chose traditional vows for their wedding, because Jessica liked the romance of being married with words others had used for years.

98° Since the guys mean the world to him, Nick's group was an obvious choice to sing "My Everything," the song he had written for Jessica.

Perfect Harmony

Music sets the mood for any occasion, and your wedding and reception are no exception. Finding good musicians can be as easy as calling a university or local concert halls, or asking friends and family for referrals. The key is to plan in advance. Call around to reception halls and ask for referrals or suggestions if you're really stumped. A last minute wedding DJ is definitely not what you're looking for.

For Jessica and Nick's wedding, music was a natural extension of the celebration, since they are both accomplished musical artists. At the ceremony, 98° performed "My Everything" for Jessica, with Nick's brother and best man, Drew, singing Nick's opening part.

Music for the ceremony itself can be vastly different from the reception music. Here, your most critical choice is in the processional piece to be played as you walk down the aisle. The more traditional choices are classics such as Pachelbel's "Canon in D," Mendelssohn's "Wedding March," and Bach's "Jesu, Joy of Man's Desiring," but you can choose any meaningful song, as long as you both find it appropriate for the occasion.

Beyond the processional, **there's much to consider when thinking about setting your dream wedding to music:**

Which style of music is your favorite as a couple? For instance, if you both like jazz, you might consider a jazz theme throughout, and use the music to create a classy, dinner-club atmosphere at your reception.

Which instruments are most appealing? Do you prefer piano or strings? Some brides and grooms prefer vocalists and soft harps, others majestic organs, and some the very classic string quartet.

What is your budget for music? If you've got limited music funds, consider using recorded music of your choice. You'll need an experienced DJ to help coordinate your choices with specifically timed moments in the reception, such as your arrival as husband and wife. Rarely do such moments occur on time, so the DJ will need to be prepared with short bits to keep the crowd occupied until the moment is right for your favorite songs.

Is the venue appropriate for your musical choice? If your reception will be held in your church's adjacent hall, a loud rock band may not be the best choice for the location. Consequently, a strolling violinist would be lost in a hall where a high school reunion is being held in an adjacent room. Confer well in advance with the reception hall's banquet director to be certain your musical choice is the best for the location.

Once you've booked the musical accompaniment to your day, you should have at least one more meeting before the wedding to review your final musical selections. This way, you can be certain your wedding music will be exactly what you expect, with your current and most up-to-date selections.

For Jessica and Nick's wedding, music was a natural extension of the celebration, since they are both accomplished musical artists. At the ceremony, 98° performed "My Everything" for Jessica, with Nick's brother and best man, Drew, singing Nick's opening part. Jessica had written a song called "My Love" for Nick, performed by the singer's writing collaborator, Trina Harmon, during the lighting of the Unity Candle.

At the end of the ceremony, a 25-voice gospel choir belted out "O Happy Day" while the newly married couple strolled down the aisle. It was a beautiful moment that was made unforgettable by the addition of a spirited, uplifting song.

For their first dance as husband and wife, Jessica and Nick danced to Van Morrison's "Crazy Love," performed by country singer Neal McCoy. The dreamy-eyed couple softly sang along. Later, Jessica and her dad, Joe, chose another Van Morrison song, "Brown-eyed Girl," for their father-daughter dance.

ACCOMPANIMENT The quartet and gospel choir at Jessica and Nick's wedding were hired through connections of the Austin chapel. Jessica's friend Trina Harmon also played piano and sang "My Love," a song written by Jessica for Nick.

FAMILY UNITY The Unity Candle was very important to Jessica and Nick, since it symbolized the uniting of their two families.

MY LOVE During the lighting of the Unity Candle, Trina Harmon sang "My Love."

An Exceptional Reception

CREATE YOUR OWN
UNFORGETTABLE POST-WEDDING CELEBRATION

MORE THAN PERFECT When Jessica walked into the reception room, her immediate response was awe. She felt that it couldn't have been more perfect.

the party of your dreams

The hallmark of a celebrity dream wedding is the sophisticated send-off of a lavish reception, complete with exotic flowers, delectable dishes, top-name musical entertainment, and all the rest of the visual trimmings your mind can imagine. Naturally, this kind of wedding reception comes with a very high price tag.

But having a gorgeous reception of your own isn't out of reach, financially speaking. There are several ways you can entertain lavishly on a budget.

For starters, you can invite fewer guests. Extended families understand that not everyone can afford to invite the whole world to share in a five-course meal. As many brides will tell you, when it comes to weddings, bigger is not always better.

You can also have a luncheon reception or choose a date that is off-peak season (October through April), since many reception halls offer discounts for their slower season.

When adding great visuals to the mix, you can always opt for a group of family and friends to decorate the hall, versus hiring a professional to do it. Get creative. You can purchase many decorative items from craft stores, and some offer discounts on bulk purchases.

Once you've got the place well decorated, you'll need to focus your energy on keeping the party moving. Here are some ways to do just that, without breaking the bank:

Keep guests active. Don't leave them standing and waiting for the next thing to happen. After the receiving line, motion them to be seated or to visit the bar. This is a good time to plan some upbeat music.

During dinner, keep the music and the wine flowing. To give guests an added opportunity for interaction, place a camera and journal at each table so that your guests can create messages for you. These can be great icebreakers for guests who are meeting for the first time, not to mention fun for you when you see them after the wedding.

Make sure your special events (like cutting the cake, tossing the bouquet or garter, and toasts from your best man and maid of honor) occur in a timely fashion. Nothing is worse for a reception than activities moving slowly, leaving the guests with nothing to do for long periods of time.

As a final note for a great reception, don't forget to include your musicians and any other professionals who helped make your wedding a success. Too often, these hard-working folks are left out of the fun because the bride forgot to include them in the original headcount given to the banquet director. It's bad etiquette to shut them out of the reception, so be sure to have at least one extra table for the people who knocked themselves out to make your dream come true.

DANCE WITH ME One of the highlights of the evening was Jessica and Nick's first dance together as husband and wife. The shimmering lights and live music made for a perfect romantic moment.

GETTING LOOSE Dancing, tossing the bouquet, and being showered in rose petals allowed Jessica and Nick to share their joy with their guests—and have an unforgettable time.

DUAL-PURPOSE UMBRELLAS With paparazzi popping out from bushes, the rain and its resulting umbrellas turned out to be blessings in disguise.

embracing the unexpected

With all the planning and preparation that went into your big day, you would think that it would be predictably perfect. The truth is, even the best-laid plans can be subject to change without notice.

Your wedding is meant to be a well-planned affair, but you should also build into it some flexibility should unexpected circumstances arise. Work your plan, but also be open to the unplanned events that will make your wedding even more memorable in the years ahead.

Even celebrity weddings can experience the stress of the unexpected. For instance, in the middle of Jessica and Nick's wedding, the October skies opened up in a surprise rain shower, forcing festivities indoors at the last minute. Fortunately for them, they had a skilled wedding planner to handle the details of the switch from an outdoor reception to an elegant indoor one. The storm even brought about some "happy accidents"; for example, the impromptu personal photo gallery of the couple that adorned a candle-lit passageway to the main reception area, and the umbrellas used by guests to keep the rain and paparazzi away.

Your wedding is meant to be a well-planned affair, but you should also build into it some flexibility should unexpected circumstances arise. Work your plan, but also be open to the unplanned events that will make your wedding even more memorable in the years ahead. Have you ever attended a wedding that had poignant or even hilarious moments that people still talk about today? Were any of those moments planned?

Despite your best efforts, you can't control every single detail of the day's events. After all the time and energy you put into your wedding planning, there comes a time when you must let go, relax and enjoy each moment as it unfolds.

THE END AND THE BEGINNING Saying goodbye at the end of the reception is a joyful moment, as it marks the beginning of a wonderful adventure together.

from this day forward

from this day forward

From the moment you take your first steps together as husband and wife, you'll be embarking on an entirely new life. From this day forward, you'll likely do everything together, from post-wedding events and thanking your guests in meaningful ways to facing an uncertain but loving future with all the potential of two worlds blended into one. In between the parties and your "happily ever after," you'll have whisked yourselves away on a fabulous (and well-deserved) honeymoon. Whether it's to a far-off, exotic location, or simply a quiet weekend away from it all, you'll likely look back at all the planning and festivities with warm, sentimental eyes.

But, alas, reality sets in the moment you return to your new home. What will happen now that you have the rest of your lives to look forward to together? How will you be able to keep the memories of your special day alive through the unpaved roads ahead? The best way to keep the dream alive is to work every day at keeping your love strong through commitment and togetherness.

For Jessica and Nick, togetherness means soulful collaboration in life and music. Both are constantly working on their own projects, but uphold their sacred bond as the priority. "We will always make time for each other," says Jessica. "Our marriage is the most important thing to both of us, and neither one of us will ever forget that."

May you feel the blessings of your sacred bond in the days ahead!

BREATHING SPACE Jessica and Nick breathed a huge sigh of relief as their wedding celebration ended and they could finally embark on their new life together.

afterglow BASK IN YOUR FIRST MOMENTS
TOGETHER AS HUSBAND AND WIFE

ALONE AT LAST Stylist Jessica Paster put the romantic finishing touches on Jessica and Nick's intimate honeymoon suite.

Romantic Getaways

The most enchanting post-wedding party is also the most private: the honeymoon. Jessica and Nick spent a fabulous 12-day honeymoon on an exotic island in Fiji, but you needn't travel to a faraway place to make your honeymoon special. Wherever you go, you should do any preparation well ahead of the wedding day.

Here are some tips to help you get ready for your first days as husband and wife:

Pack ahead of time. At least one week before the wedding, pack your bags and be ready to roll. That way, packing won't be an afterthought, and you'll stand a much better chance of packing everything you'll need.

Designate one of your attendants to pick up any gifts, clothing, etc. you've brought with you to the wedding and reception. You'll want to make a clean break for it after your final dance, and you can't do that as easily when you have to walk around the reception hall rounding up your stuff.

Ask a groomsman (typically the best man) to return the groom's tuxedo. Have one of your attendants take your wedding gown to the cleaners to be cleaned and preserved.

Confirm travel plans a week before the wedding. Since the groom may not be as busy as the bride-to-be, put travel confirmations on his "to-do" list. The groom could also take care of any traveler's checks or foreign currency exchanges in the week before the wedding.

Pack your address book. If you want to send postcards from your destination, you'll need to have addresses handy.

Don't forget to pack special touches. Romantic honeymoons can include scented candles, silk lingerie and two lush, velvety robes. It can also be as simple as including customized CDs with all of your favorite music.

Finally, get some rest before you depart for your honeymoon location. A good night's sleep in a hotel the night before you leave for your trip will ensure a relaxing, stress-free honeymoon, and will help you recover from the intensity of your wedding day.

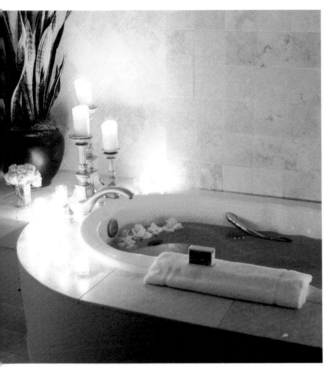

ROMANTIC INTERLUDE Not only was the room and its warm bath illuminated in sensual candles, but Paster also arranged for hors d'oeuvres and other wedding delectables to be waiting for the happy couple.

INTERVIEW WITH TRAVEL AGENT *Lenora Foster*

Lenora Foster of Dallas' Landmark Travel helped Jessica and Nick plan their honeymoon escape. "They came to me with three places in mind," she says. "Mostly, they wanted a place to get away from it all, relax and just hang out."

Ultimately, the couple chose the secluded and very private Turtle Island of Fiji for their honeymoon destination. "The staff at Turtle Island really caters to the 18 couples who are permitted on the island at one time," says Foster. "There's fine dining, private beach picnics, horseback riding, and snorkeling, among many other activities. It really suited their need to relax and have fun."

"You can spend hours on the Internet and still not find what you want," Foster says. She advises newlyweds to work with an experienced travel agent "to get the best deals" and to find the best destination fit for them.

Should you go it alone, seeking travel packages on the Internet? "You can spend hours on the Internet and still not find what you want," Foster says. She advises newlyweds to work with an experienced travel agent "to get the best deals" and to find the best destination fit for them. "Know what your budget is, and then balance that with what you like to do. Do you prefer large crowds or privacy? Are you flexible in your travel arrangements or looking to travel at a specific time of year? All of these things should be taken into account by your travel agent."

MEMORY QUILT Personalized well wishes from dear friends are captured forever in each square of Jessica and Nick's wedding quilt.

Preserving memories

Jessica and Nick's wedding included many personal touches aimed at preserving the memory of their special day. Aside from the wedding photographs that carefully captured each romantic detail of the day, the one memory-preserver that stood out as intimate, heartfelt and sincere was the bridal quilt.

Guests were sent a patch of quilt on which to write or embroider their personal well wishes to the bride and groom. They sent the patches in with their RSVPs, and then the quilt was sewn and framed for display along a wall at the reception.

We thought the quilt was an adorable idea. This is something we'll have the rest of our lives.—JS

You can easily create a bridal quilt of many wishes for your wedding.
Purchase quilting squares from a fabric or craft store, mail them with your invites, and then have a friend or relative sew the pieces together into a quilt that will keep you safe and warm for all the days of your life together.

Guests were sent a patch of quilt on which to write their personal well wishes to the bride and groom. They sent the patches in with their RSVPs, and then the quilt was sewn and framed for display along a wall at the reception.

Other ways to keep the memories alive:

Store a piece of wedding cake in your freezer so that you can eat some on your first anniversary.

Buy two identical garters—one to toss and one to keep in your scrapbook.

Keep your Unity Candle for relighting on your anniversaries.

Enlarge and frame your favorite wedding photo. You can pay to have this done professionally, or do it at a frame-it-yourself shop.

Send a photo of each guest (taken with the cameras left at each table) in your thank-you card.

There are limitless creative ways to preserve your wedding memories. If you feel overwhelmed by details, ask a close friend or relative to help.

happily ever after

A NEW CHAPTER IN YOUR
LIFE TOGETHER BEGINS NOW

a final wish

FROM JESSICA

The beauty of love expresses itself throughout many faiths. Something that was read at my wedding and may be read at yours is St. Paul's famous letter to the Corinthians. It is one of my favorite passages about love:

Love is patient, love is kind. It does not envy, it does not boast, it is not proud. It is not rude, it is not self-seeking, it is not easily angered, it keeps no record of wrongs. Love does not delight in evil but rejoices with the truth. It always protects, always trusts, always hopes, always perseveres. Love never fails. *—1 Corinthians 13:1*

Love is the most powerful human emotion, and your wedding celebrates that love. Whether you've been planning it for six months or for sixteen years, this day holds the promise of a lifetime of happiness.

For most of you who have read and reflected upon the chapters of my wedding experience, saying "I do" is just around the corner. Through all of the chaos and excitement, I urge you to sit back and enjoy the gift of love you have received. I wish you all a lifetime of beautiful wedding memories.

Resources

For more information on how to make your wedding everything you've ever wanted, consult these additional resources:

Consultants

PHOTOGRAPHY:

Joe Buissink
JOE BUISSINK INC.
Beverly Hills, CA
310/360-0198
joebuissink.com

Ashley Garmon
ASHLEY GARMON
PHOTOGRAPHERS
Austin, TX
512/458-3358
ashleygarmonphoto.com

MAKEUP:

Ulli Schober
THE CELESTINE AGENCY
Santa Monica, CA
310/998-1977
celestineagency.com

Karan Mitchell
LUXE MANAGEMENT
Los Angeles, CA
323/856-8540
luxemgmt.com
kjmhotshot@aol.com

MANICURES:

Melissa Bozant Washington
EPICUREUS PETITE SPA
Beverly Hills, CA
323/653-6373
epicureuspetitespa.com

HAIR:

Ken Pavés
PAVÉS SALON & SPAS
Los Angeles, CA
586/416-8600
pavesprofessional.com

Rita Hazan
ADIR
New York, NY
212/734-4757

TRAVEL:

Lenora Foster
LANDMARK TRAVEL SERVICES
Dallas, TX
800/747-9484
landmarktraveler.com

FLOWERS:

Mark Held
MARK'S GARDEN
Sherman Oaks, CA
818/906-1718

CAKE:

Sam Godfrey
PERFECT ENDINGS
Napa, CA
707/259-0500
perfectendings.com

DRESS:

Vera Wang
VERA WANG BRIDAL SALON
New York, NY
212/628-3400
verawang.com

WEDDING PLANNING:

Mindy Weiss
MINDY WEISS PARTY
CONSULTANTS
Beverly Hills, CA
310/205-6000
mindyweiss.com

SIGNATURE SOIREES
Los Angeles, CA
818/773-7828
signature-soirees.com

STYLIST:

Jessica Paster
LUXE MANAGEMENT
Los Angeles, CA
323/856-8540
luxemgmt.com

JEWELRY:

Carol Brodie
HARRY WINSTON
Beverly Hills, CA
800/988-4110
harry-winston.com

BRIDESMAIDS' GIFTS:

Jaye Hershe
INTUITION
Los Angeles, CA
877/310-8442

Books

WEDDING PLANNING:

Budget Wedding Sourcebook by Madeline Barillo. (McGraw-Hill/Contemporary Books, 2000). A book that proves you can have a memorable, even fabulous wedding on a budget.

Best Friend's Guide to Planning a Wedding by Laura Webb Carrigan. (Regan Books, 2001). Your "best friend" and advice guide to planning your wedding.

Great Wedding Tips from the Experts: What Every Bride Can Learn from the Most Successful Wedding Planners by Robbi Ernst. (McGraw-Hill/Contemporary Books, 2000). Shower and wedding tips from a professional wedding planner.

Priceless Weddings for Under $5,000 by Kathleen Kennedy. (Three Rivers Press, 2000). Once you set some goals, you'll be ready to work on the budget. Here's a guide to doing more with much less.

Easy Wedding Planner by Elizabeth Lluch. (National Book Network, 2000). A simple, straightforward guide to planning the wedding of your dreams.

Vera Wang on Weddings by Vera Wang. (Harper Collins, 2001). A comprehensive ideas manual reflecting decades of wedding experience from Jessica's dress designer.

PHOTOGRAPHY

Innovative Techniques for Wedding Photography by David Neil Arndt. (Amherst Media, 2000). Tips on how to keep your wedding pictures alive and well for years to come.

The Art of Wedding Photography: Professional Techniques with Style by Bambi Cantrell. (Watson-Guptill Publications, 2000). A lovely book compiled by an award-winning wedding photographer, full of tips and good direction.

DECORATIONS

Handcrafted Weddings: Over 100 Projects and Ideas for Personalizing Your Wedding (Creative Publishing International, 1999). Great ways to create a warm, romantic wedding with personally designed decorations.

Creative Wedding Decorations You Can Make edited by Teresa Nelson. (Betterway Publications, 1998). Feeling creative? Want a more personal touch? This book will help you create fabulous wedding decorations, saving you lots of money.

FOOD

Bride and Groom's First Cookbook by Abigail Kirsch. (Main Street Books, 1996). A helpful guide to post-wedding meal planning, including tips and menus.

Cater Your Own Wedding by Michael Flowers. (New Page Books, 2000). Great examples of menus that will rival even the most discriminating professional caterer's.

The Honeymoon's Over...So What's for Dinner? by Maria Vick. (Vantage Press, 2001). Even the best couples can't live on love alone; here's a culinary guide to "feed the flame."

MISCELLANEOUS

Best Wedding Shower Book: A Complete Guide for Party Planners by Courtney Cook. (Meadowbrook, 2001). Great ideas for how to plan (and survive) your bridal shower.

Complete Book of Wedding Vows by Diane Warner. (Career Press, 1996). Hundreds of ways to say, "I do."

Engagement and Wedding Rings: The Definitive Buying Guide for People in Love by Antoinette Matlins. (Gemstone Press, 1999). Fabulous rings are the stuff of dreams, and this book is full of gorgeous designs for every budget.

Emily Post's Weddings by Peggy Post. (HarperResource, 1999). Answers to all of your wedding etiquette questions.

Magazines

Bride's (bi-monthly). A terrific resource for planning and idea-gathering.

InStyle Weddings (quarterly). The trend-setting publication for weddings with panache. Read the romantic stories of celebrities in love, and get some great tips on how to incorporate some of their brightest wedding elements into your nuptials at a fraction of the cost.

Modern Bride (monthly). A classic, must-read for articles, tips, ideas and photos. Usually features a tear-out planning worksheet.

The Knot (quarterly). What's hot, what's not—with lots of tips, photos, and more.

Websites

Visit any of the following online resources for the latest wedding tips, services and links to other helpful sites:

instyle.com
theknot.com
thebigday.com
weddingchannel.com
planyourwedding.net
honeyluna.com

Credits

Concept | Jessica Simpson, Tina Simpson

Writer | Katina Z. Jones

Editor | Karen Keenan
NVU PRODUCTIONS

Art Director & Designer | Sara Frampton
NVU PRODUCTIONS

Photography

Photographer | JOE BUISSINK
Pages 1, 2-3, 4, 6, 10-11, 14, 15, 17, 22-23, 25-31, 32-33, 35, 39-41, 42-47, 50-51, 53, 54-55, 59, 64, 65, 71, 72-73, 74, 84, 86-87, 88, 90-93, 97-102, 104-109, 110, 112-115, 119, 120, 122, 123, 124, 125, 127, 129, 130-131, 133, 134-135, 136, 137, 138, 139, 140-143, 144, 145-151, 152, 153, 154, 155-156, 159-161, 164, 166-171
Camera Assistant | Gail Chatelain
Album Designer | Urbanie Lucero
Studio Manager | Kristen Meagher

Photographer | ASHLEY GARMON
Associate Photographer | EMILY JOYCE
Pages 5, 9, 12-13, 14, 17, 18-21, 32, 34, 35, 36-38, 42, 53, 56-57, 59, 60-63, 65, 67, 68-69, 70, 74, 75-83, 84, 88, 94, 103, 110, 111, 116-117, 119, 120, 121, 122, 123, 124, 127, 128, 133, 136, 138, 144, 152, 154, 162-163, 165

Photographer | CRISTIANA CEPPAS
Pages 5, 6, 16, 24, 52, 58, 66, 118, 126, 132
Camera Assistants | Todd Semo, T. J. Chrume, Kirstie Tweed
Prop Stylist | Michi Okimoto
Makeup Stylists | David Michaud, Betten Chaston
Location Scout | Greg Robinson

Photographer | NIGEL BARKER
Pages 5, 48

Photographer | MATTHEW MENDENHALL
Page 6

Dream Makers / Consultants Involved with Wedding

Floral Designers | Mark Held, Joseph Arias | MARK'S GARDEN
Wedding Planner | Mindy Weiss
Pastry Chefs | Sam Godfrey, Michael Martin | PERFECT ENDINGS
Hairstylist | Ken Pavés
Haircolorist | Rita Hazan
Makeup Artists | Ulli Schober, Karan Mitchell
Manicurist | Melissa Bozant Washington
Stylist | Jessica Paster
Dress Designers | Vera Wang, Robert Barnowski

Wedding Party | Devon Biere, Brian Bonecutter, Lisa Christensen, Tony Christensen, Gavin Gleason, Jay Goodlett, Andre Henson, Jessie Rice Holliday, Justin Jeffre, Drew Lachey, Isaac Lachey, Lea Lachey, Andrea Lee, Stephanie McGuire, Jessica Cooper Melker, Lesa Neff, Ashlee Simpson, Robin Johnson Webb.

Ring Bearer, Flower Girls | Nick Biere, Meghan Goodlett, Kia Henson

Book and DVD Production

NVU PRODUCTIONS
Project Coordinator | Cara Carney
Interactive Designer | John Fuller
Video Editor | Michael Lister
Internet Developer | Andrew Falconer
Production Manager | Melinda Fry
President | Jim Forni
Chief Creative Officer | Tom O'Grady

Prepress | RESOURCE GRAPHIC, INC.
Printer | INNERWORKINGS, LLC

Jessica's Thank-yous

First, I want to thank God for blessing this world with the universal emotion of love. Thank you for listening to the prayers of my soul and for blessing me with my Prince Charming. Which leads me to my soul mate, my husband, Nick. I love you more every day. Even when I feel like my love for you has filled every inch of my heart, somehow there is even more love tomorrow.

TO MY FAMILY:

Mom | This book would have never happened without your support and ideas. Thank you for being right by my side during every beautiful experience. I love you.

Dad | I love you so much. I'm so proud to have such a wonderful man as a father. Thank you for teaching me about true love. You don't have to let go.

Ashlee | My maid of honor and my best friend. I love you so much.

To all the rest of you, thank you for all of your prayers that led me to the man of my dreams.

Nana and Papaw | 50 years…wow. Y'all inspire Nick and me every day.

To my new family | I am so excited to be a part of such a wonderful family. Thank you for all of the prayers that led Nicholas to me.

In loving memory of Curtis and Joyce Simpson (Papa and Nanny) and Robert Fopma (Grandpa). Your presence was felt on our special day. We love you.

Friends | Thank you for your love and support.

Jim, Cara, Sara, Karen | Thank you for making dreams come true.

Katina | Thank you for investing your heart and words. You have made everything so special.

Publisher's Dedication

Few events in life compete with "the wedding day" for significance. Perhaps none are as well chronicled in our photographs, video and memories. When I first met with Jessica Simpson and her mother Tina, I knew there was a desire to go beyond memorializing a life-changing event to experiencing the complete celebration from conception through execution. With true Southern graciousness, Jessica presents her first book, together with all the wedding experts that helped make her day so extraordinary.

In parallel fashion, creative credit for *I Do* goes to a collective. The first and foremost credit goes to the Simpson family. What began as a concept with Jessica and her supportive parents, Joe and Tina, was made a reality by a group of committed creative partners. Many thanks to the core creative contributors of the book: Joe Buissink, Ashley Garmon, and Cristiana Ceppas for their stunning original photography and Katina Jones for the principal writing of the text.

A substantial measure of gratitude must be extended to NVU's team for performing superbly in rendering a book and DVD despite a compressed schedule. Kudos to all of you, for tireless dedication from start to finish. In the end, you had no rehearsal; you all got it right on the big day. Thank you.

As always, thanks to NVU's key supporters; Brad Berkley, Pat Forni, Jim Lillie and Bob Murray, who constitute the unseen spine of all NVU Editions.

James T. Forni
President & Publisher
NVU EDITIONS